**W9-ACM-744**

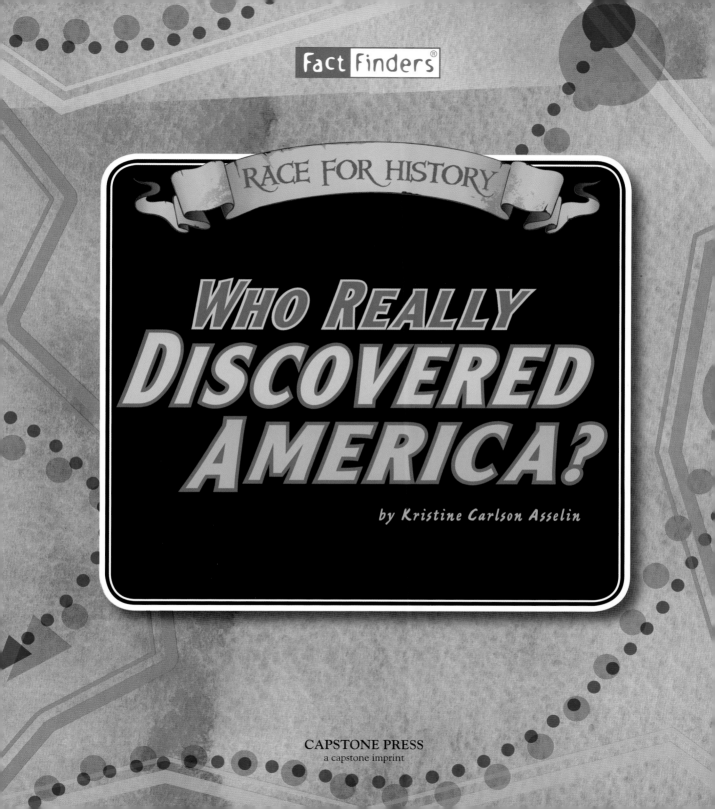

Fact Finders®

RACE FOR HISTORY

# WHO REALLY DISCOVERED AMERICA?

by Kristine Carlson Asselin

CAPSTONE PRESS
a capstone imprint

Fact Finders are published by Capstone Press,
151 Good Counsel Drive, P.O. Box 669, Mankato, Minnesota 56002.
www.capstonepub.com

Books published by Capstone Press are manufactured with paper
containing at least 10 percent post-consumer waste.

*Library of Congress Cataloging-in-Publication Data*
Asselin, Kristine Carlson.
Who really discovered America? / by Kristine Carlson Asselin.
p. cm.—(Fact finders. Race for history)
Includes bibliographical references and index.
Summary: "Follows the stories of ancient nomads, Leif Eriksson, and Christopher Columbus as they make their
way to a new land we now call America"—Provided by publisher.
ISBN 978-1-4296-3342-0 (library binding)
ISBN 978-1-4296-6247-5 (paperback)
1. America—Discovery and exploration—Juvenile literature. 2. Explorers—America—History—Juvenile literature.
I. Title. II. Series.
E101.A83 2011
970.01—dc22                                                                                    2010031216

**Editorial Credits**
Jennifer Besel, editor; Alison Thiele, series designer; Bobbie Nuytten, book designer;
    Wanda Winch, media researcher; Eric Manske, production specialist

**Photo Credits**
Alamy: Mary Evans Picture Library, 6, North Winds Picture Archives, 10, 15; The Art Archive/National
Anthropological Museum Mexico/Gianni Dagli Orti, cover (top left), 5 (top), 12; The Bridgeman Art Library/©Look
and Learn/Private Collection/Ron Embleton, cover (bottom), 5 (bottom); ©Canadian Museum of Civilization,
Canada's Visual History, V53, IMG2008-0007-1576-Dm, 25; Getty Images: The Bridgeman Art Library, cover
(top right), 5 (middle), The Bridgeman Art Library/Angus McBride, 16, Hulton Archive/Archive Photos, 21; The
Granger Collection, New York, 9; Library of Congress: Prints and Photographs Division, 22; Nova Development
Corporation, 28-29 (all); Simon Fraser University: Museum of Archaeology & Ethnology, 18

**Capstone Press thanks Dr. Barbara J. Winter, Director of the Museum of Archaeology and Ethnology
at Simon Fraser University, for her assistance with this book.**

Printed in the United States of America in Stevens Point, Wisconsin.

072011       006285R

# TABLE OF CONTENTS

THE RACE . . . . . . . . . . . . . . . . . . . . . . . . . . 4

Chapter 1 *LEAVING FOR A NEW WORLD* . . . . . 6
Chapter 2 *STARTLING DISCOVERIES* . . . . . . . . 12
Chapter 3 *EXPLORING A NEW LAND* . . . . . . . 18

THE WINNER . . . . . . . . . . . . . . . . . . . . . . . . 24

TIMELINE . . . . . . . . . . . . . . . . . . . . . . . . . . 28
GLOSSARY . . . . . . . . . . . . . . . . . . . . . . . . . . 30
READ MORE . . . . . . . . . . . . . . . . . . . . . . . . . 31
INTERNET SITES . . . . . . . . . . . . . . . . . . . . . . 31
INDEX . . . . . . . . . . . . . . . . . . . . . . . . . . . . . 32

# THE RACE

The areas now called North and South America were among the last territories to be explored by humans. The land was wild and unknown. And it was surrounded by miles of unpredictable oceans.

The journey to discover this untamed land was dangerous and long. And the reasons to explore it were many. Some people were looking for a safer, more comfortable place to live. Others went for adventure. And some raced to prove an idea.

Men and women battled the weather, wild animals, and stormy seas. They left their homes to endure dangerous journeys. But there can only be one winner. Who really discovered America?

**nomadic:** wandering from place to place

**Viking:** a member of a fierce group of warriors

# MEET THE PLAYERS

**ANCIENT SIBERIANS**

A small tribe of **nomadic** hunters from more than 12,000 years ago—they make their home in the cold mountains of Siberia. The tribe hunts woolly mammoths for their meat and fur.

**CHRISTOPHER COLUMBUS**

A religious, 41-year-old man—he was born in Italy, but now in the 1490s lives in Spain. He's an experienced sailor who has sailed to many places including the Canary Islands, near Africa.

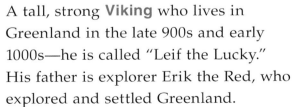

**LEIF ERIKSSON**

A tall, strong **Viking** who lives in Greenland in the late 900s and early 1000s—he is called "Leif the Lucky." His father is explorer Erik the Red, who explored and settled Greenland.

# CHAPTER ONE
# LEAVING FOR A NEW WORLD

Woolly mammoths were the ancient people's main source of food.

## Ancient Siberians on the Move

It's more than 12,000 years ago. A tribe of men, women, and children live high in the cold Siberian mountains. The tribe's hunters leave for days, searching for woolly mammoths. Because mammoths are huge, a catch means meat for everyone. But lately, the hunters cannot find mammoths. Tribe members gather roots and berries to eat, but it's not enough. Everyone goes to bed hungry.

The tribe's people know they won't survive if they stay in the mountains. The hunters hear from another tribe about herds of mammoths far to the east. The tribe decides to go east to find the herds.

Mothers wrap their babies and lift them onto their backs. The hunters pack their small stone tools. Everyone dresses in animal skins for warmth. Carrying their stone-tipped spears, the hunters lead the tribe out of the mountains. They walk toward unknown land. It will be a long, hard trip. They doubt everyone will live to see the end of the journey.

RACE FACT

Archaeologists believe the tribe probably had no more than 50 members.

## Eriksson's Mission

A group of Vikings have lived in Greenland for about 15 years now. But they are explorers at heart. A few years ago, a sailor named Bjarni claimed to have seen strange new lands. He and his crew had sailed off course on their way to Greenland. The crew wanted to explore the new lands. But Bjarni decided to sail on. Many people think Bjarni should have stopped to investigate the discovery.

Now in AD 1000, the Viking leaders decide to send someone to explore the lands Bjarni saw. They might make good settlements. Leif Eriksson is chosen to lead 35 men on this exploration. He has experience as a warrior and explorer. Eriksson knows the trip will be dangerous. In fact, he and his crew may never see their families again. But Eriksson is too curious about what he will find to back out. Eriksson boards his **knorr** for the journey to unknown lands.

Eriksson and his crew on the ship

**knorr:** a type of ship used by Vikings

Columbus (left) explaining his plans to the king and queen of Spain

## Columbus' Goal

It's 1492 in Spain. Christopher Columbus is not looking for a new land. Instead, he thinks he can find a quicker way to get to an old one. He believes it's possible to sail west from Europe to China instead of walking east over land. **Exotic** spices and rare silk come from China. People pay lots of money for those things. He will be rewarded well if his ideas are right. But he's had a hard time convincing others his plans will work.

Columbus asked leaders in Portugal, France, and England to pay for his trip. They all refused. For the last five years, he's asked the king and queen of Spain for help over and over. Now in April 1492, they have finally agreed to pay for his voyage in return for most of the riches he promises to find.

They give him two ships, the *Niña* and the *Pinta*. Columbus buys a third ship himself, which he names *Santa María*. He hires a crew of 90 men to sail with him. Certain of success, Columbus boards the *Santa María* to begin the journey of a lifetime.

**RACE FACT**
Life onboard the ships was not a vacation. The crews had to keep the boats' sails working and pump out water that washed aboard. They ate a stew of salted fish and biscuits crawling with maggots.

**exotic:** from a faraway place

# Ancient Siberians' Dangerous Crossing

As the ancient Siberians walk in unknown territory, they know this is the journey of a lifetime. Frozen glaciers cover much of the land. The ocean's water is frozen in thick slabs of ice. Large grassy plains stretch far and wide between the glaciers.

The wind whips around them as they walk on the grassy **steppe**. The rocky land is hard on their feet. They walk close together, protecting each other from wild animals and cold temperatures. Separation from the group would mean certain death.

The tribe sees wolves and saber-toothed cats in this foreign land. Finally, they spot a herd of woolly mammoths grazing in the distance. The hunters are able to get meat for everyone. But when the mammoths move away, the tribe must follow. They are very far from their mountain home. But keeping near the mammoths means they will not go hungry.

Soon, tribe members hear the sound of gushing water. It gets louder as they approach. The children cover their ears. But the sight of the raging river is worse than the sound. The water roars down a mountain glacier, surging into the valley below. The mammoths are nowhere to be seen, but they must have crossed the river. How will the tribe get across? And what is waiting on the other side?

The ancient people carried all their belongings on the long, hard journey.

**steppe:** a huge, treeless plain

# Eriksson's Discoveries

Eriksson and his men have no idea what they'll find across the ocean. They are prepared for anything. Each man travels with a bow and arrow, an axe, and a sword.

Eriksson uses Bjarni's descriptions of the lands to guide their journey. When the wind is too weak to fill the sails, the men row. They are strong and used to this exhausting task. After a week of sailing, they spot land. They make landfall on the strange rocky ground. But they don't stay long. As they sail farther south, they see land with trees. In their excitement, they row harder. They stop and explore a bit here too.

Soon they are back in the boats. Bjarni had seen three different lands. So the Vikings sail south again in hopes of finding more land. Two days later, they come upon a beautiful island. The landscape is lush and green. When they go ashore, the men drink dew from the grass. It tastes wonderful.

The island is amazing, but winter is coming. Eriksson must make a decision. If they want to return to Greenland, they must leave now to beat the stormy winter seas. If they stay on the island, they can return to Greenland with a full report in the spring. But spending the winter here means being away from their families even longer. And they have no idea what weather they will have to survive if they stay. Eriksson must decide what to do—quickly.

Eriksson and his men rowed ashore to explore the lands.

**RACE FACT** Eriksson named the first land they found Helluland, meaning "Stone-slab Land." He named the second land Markland which means "Forest Land."

Columbus' men were overjoyed when they learned that land was near.

## Columbus' Surprise

At sea, Columbus faces a decision that could destroy any hope of achieving his goal. The ships have sailed quickly through the calm ocean. They have traveled very far. In fact, the crew thinks they've gone too far.

No other ship has gone so long without seeing land. The men believe they're too far from home to get back safely. At first, they whisper of throwing Columbus overboard so they can turn around. Soon the whispers turn to shouts. Columbus has to decide what to do. He doesn't want to turn back. But he doesn't want to die either. Columbus tells the crew they will turn back if they don't see land in three days.

That very night, sticks and plants float by the boat—evidence of land. Every crew member strains his eyes to the horizon. They have been at sea 33 days when a lookout on the *Pinta* shouts, "Land!"

As the sun rises, the men survey the beach ahead of them. They see small huts and naked people. This is not how they imagined the booming land of China. Columbus wonders where this dangerous journey has taken them.

**RACE FACT**

The crew had no sleeping quarters onboard the ships. They had to sleep on the deck. During storms, they crowded below deck with the rats and lice.

## CHAPTER THREE
# EXPLORING A NEW LAND

The ancient people sailed along the coast in animal skin boats.

# The Ancient Siberians Find a Home

The ancient Siberians have no idea where this dangerous journey will take them. But they have survived so far. The great river will not beat them. A hunter tries to cross on foot, but the current quickly washes him downstream. He manages to pull himself out. But most people wouldn't be so lucky.

A small group sets out to find a way around the water. Days later, the group returns with news. Farther downstream the river pours into a vast ocean. The remains of a giant whale lay on the shore. The rest of the tribe follows the group to see the amazing sight. Finally, they see bones rising from the rocky shore. This animal was bigger than any mammoth they have ever seen.

Looking at the bones, the oldest woman in the tribe remembers watching her grandfather make a boat from animal bones and skins. If they could make a boat with these bones, they could float across the water. The rest of the tribe has never seen a boat. But this is the best idea they have. They use the whale's ribs as the boat's frame. Then they stretch walrus hides over the ribs. Carefully, they test the skin boat. It works! Soon, they make enough boats for everyone.

The tribe sails south along the foreign coast. They search for a place to settle. On the way, they stop at areas that have escaped the ice. There, they find plants and small animals to eat. Eventually, the tribe discovers that whale and seal are good substitutes for mammoth meat. They decide to settle near the ocean. The tribe has found a new and plentiful place to live.

# Eriksson Names the Land

Eriksson believes this new land could be a plentiful place to live. He makes a decision. He and his men will stay here for the winter. They came to explore, and that's what they will do.

The Vikings build large wooden houses for protection and warmth. They eat salmon, berries, and herbs. The winter isn't too cold. They are able to explore hundreds of miles of territory.

Eriksson doesn't think anyone else has ever been here. He decides to name this new land. He calls it "Vinland" for the wild grapes that grow here.

When winter is over, the Vikings prepare to return home. They cut down trees and collect grapes. They load these things in the knorrs and set sail. When they arrive, the Greenland colonists are excited about new sources of timber and grapes for making wine.

Vikings travel to Vinland many times to establish a new colony. But on one of these trips, men in animal skin boats are waiting. The **native** people attack the surprised Vikings. Many on both sides are injured in the battle.

The Vikings and natives battle many times over the land. The Vikings don't know where the natives came from. But they don't want to live in fear of attack. Finally, the Vikings abandon hope of settling Vinland and return to Greenland.

**native:** a person who originally lived in an area

Many people died in the battles between the natives and Vikings.

**RACE FACT**

The Vikings called the natives "skraelings." Historians believe that word meant "scared or scruffy one."

## Columbus Claims the Land

Columbus does not abandon hope. He believes he has landed on an island near China. As the native people watch, Columbus claims the island for Spain, then drops to his knees in prayer.

Then he turns his attention to the natives. He calls them "Indians" because he believes he's in the East Indies. Columbus gives the natives glass beads and other trinkets. They like the presents and bring Columbus parrots and gifts in return.

For several months Columbus and his crew explore the island and others nearby. They search for gold or other valuable items. Finally, Columbus returns to Spain to tell of his discovery. He is a hero. He parades down the street in his finest clothes. The six natives he brought back with him amaze the crowds. Columbus tells everyone that he has found a western route to China.

**RACE FACT** Columbus brought back several things that Europeans had never seen before, including hammocks, pineapples, and parrots.

Columbus (center) and his crew after landing

# THE WINNER

Three separate groups landed on American soil at three different times in history. So who really discovered America?

The winner is the ancient Siberians. Ancient people crossed the Pacific Ocean from Siberia during the **Ice Age**. The land looked very different then. Much of the land and sea was frozen in ice. But there were areas along the coast that escaped the ice. These places, called refugia, had plants and animals living there. The ancient people floated in boats along the coast, stopping at refugia to gather food. Eventually, they settled on the western coast of what is now Alaska. Over time, their **descendants** spread farther south over North and South America.

Exactly when these ancient people came and how they lived is still a puzzle. Scientists don't know what these people called themselves, either. Because they were first to the Americas, archaeologists often call them ancient Americans.

**Ice Age:** a period of time in history when much of Earth was covered in ice

**descendant:** a person's child and the members of a family born after that child

The ancient Americans built homes and settled on the North American coast.

Leif Eriksson and the Vikings explored parts of northeastern Canada in the early 1000s. Many archaeologists believe the Vikings settled in the area now called Newfoundland. The Vikings were the first Europeans in America. But they weren't the first people there.

After the first Siberians settled on the Alaskan coast, several other tribes made their way from Siberia into present-day Canada. Descendants of these tribes discovered the area long before the Vikings. In fact, they were the people who fought the Vikings and drove them from the island.

By the time Columbus arrived, millions of people lived in the Americas. Columbus landed on an island in the Caribbean Sea in 1492. When he died in 1506, he still thought the island was close to China. Today we know that he was nowhere near China. He didn't achieve his goal of finding a western route to China. But his landing was the beginning of European exploration of the New World.

Descendants of the ancient Americans actually greeted Columbus when he arrived on the island. So why does Columbus usually get credit for discovering America? When the Siberians arrived on American soil, they didn't know they had discovered a new land. They simply migrated to where they could find food. In Columbus' time, he had more opportunity to share the story of his voyage. And at that time, most Europeans believed they were superior to the natives. So even though there were people there, the European newcomers claimed they had discovered America. And that idea was recorded in the history books.

The ancient Siberians were the first humans to step onto American soil. However, we only know their story through discoveries of tools and bones. Archaeological sites continue to give clues about these ancient people. So the race to discover America is over. But the race to learn about the people who discovered it continues today.

SIBERIA

ALASKA

PACIFIC OCEAN

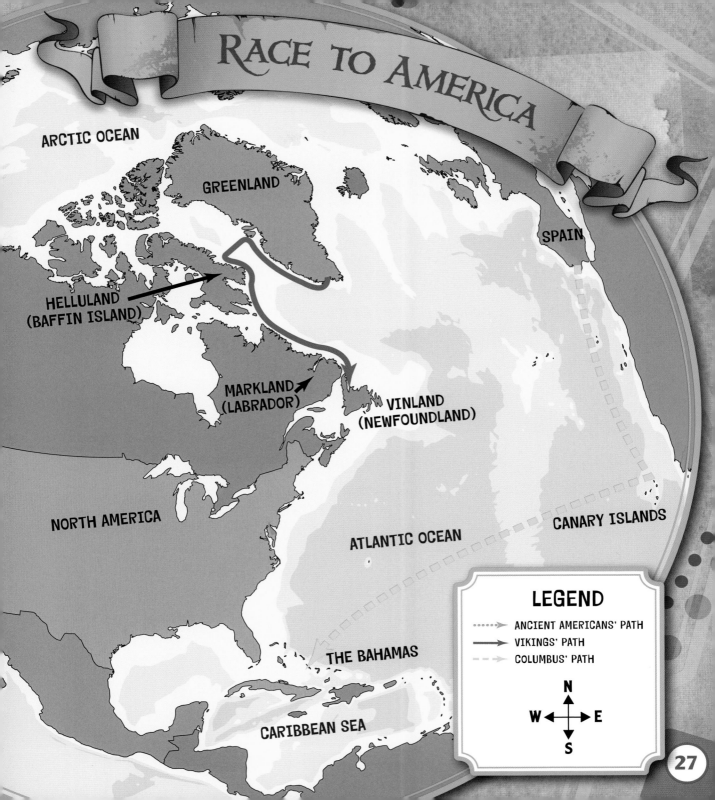

# RACE TO AMERICA

ARCTIC OCEAN

GREENLAND

SPAIN

HELLULAND
(BAFFIN ISLAND)

MARKLAND
(LABRADOR)

VINLAND
(NEWFOUNDLAND)

NORTH AMERICA

CANARY ISLANDS

ATLANTIC OCEAN

THE BAHAMAS

CARIBBEAN SEA

## LEGEND

- ········▷ ANCIENT AMERICANS' PATH
- ───▶ VIKINGS' PATH
- ╌╌▷ COLUMBUS' PATH

N
W · E
S

# TIMELINE

**25,000–14,000 BC**
Lower sea levels exist during the last Ice Age. Large areas of grassy plains are exposed between Siberia and Alaska.

**AD 1000**
Leif Eriksson and the Vikings establish a settlement called Vinland in what is now Newfoundland, Canada.

**25,000 BC**

**AROUND 17,000 BC**
The ancient Siberians walk out of the mountains of Siberia and sail down what is now the northwest coast of the United States.

**1020** The Vikings abandon Vinland after several battles with natives.

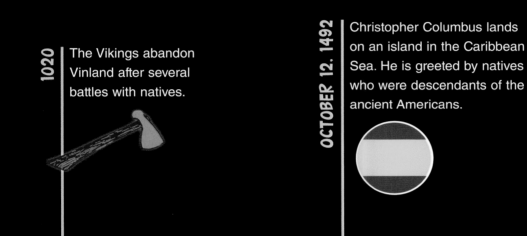

**OCTOBER 12. 1492** Christopher Columbus lands on an island in the Caribbean Sea. He is greeted by natives who were descendants of the ancient Americans.

AD 1493

**AUGUST 3. 1492** Christopher Columbus leaves Spain with three ships, the *Niña*, *Pinta*, and *Santa María*.

**MARCH 15. 1493** Christopher Columbus returns to Spain with six natives and treasures that had never been seen before.

# GLOSSARY

**archaeologist** (ar-kee-OL-uh-jist)—a scientist who studies how people lived in the past

**descendant** (di-SEN-duhnt)—a person's child and the generations of a family born after that child

**exotic** (eg-ZOT-ik)—strange, fascinating, and from a faraway place

**Ice Age** (EYESS AJE)—a period of time in history when much of Earth was covered by ice

**knorr** (NOR)—a type of ship used by Vikings to move people, cargo, or animals across the ocean

**native** (NAY-tiv)—a person who originally lived in a particular place or area

**nomadic** (noh-MAD-ik)—wandering from place to place

**steppe** (STEP)—vast, treeless plains

**Viking** (VYE-king)—a member of a fierce group of warriors and pirates who invaded Europe from the 700s to about 1100; the Vikings were from Scandinavia, an area in Europe including present-day Norway, Sweden, and Denmark

# READ MORE

**Freedman, Russell.** *Who Was First?: Discovering the Americas.* New York: Clarion Books, 2007.

**Leavitt, Amie Jane.** *Christopher Columbus.* What's So Great About—? Hockessin, Del.: Mitchell Lane Publishers, 2008.

**Macdonald, Fiona.** *Vikings.* Remarkable Man and Beast— Facing Survival. Broomall, Penn.: Mason Crest., 2011.

**Wyatt, Valerie.** *Who Discovered America?* Toronto: Kid's Can Press, 2008.

# INTERNET SITES

FactHound offers a safe, fun way to find Internet sites related to this book. All of the sites on FactHound have been researched by our staff.

Here's all you do:

Visit *www.facthound.com*

Type in this code: 9781429633420

Super-cool stuff!

Check out projects, games and lots more at
**www.capstonekids.com**

# INDEX

ancient Siberians, 5, 7, 13, 19, 24, 26
    boats, 19, 24
    descendants of, 24, 26
    hunting, 5, 7, 13
    weapons, 7

Columbus, Christopher, 5, 11, 17, 23, 26
Columbus' 1492 expedition
    crew, 11, 17
    discoveries of, 17, 23, 26
    goals of, 11
    problems of, 11, 17
    ships, 11, 17

Eriksson, Leif, 5, 8, 14, 15, 20, 25
Eriksson's 1000 expedition
    crew, 8, 20
    discoveries, 14, 15, 20
    knorrs, 8, 14, 20
    weapons, 14

Greenland, 5, 8, 14, 20

Ice Age, 24

Newfoundland, 25

Spain, 5, 11, 23

Vikings, 5, 8, 20, 21, 25
    and exploration, 5, 8
Vinland, 20
    battles for, 20

woolly mammoths, 5, 7, 13, 19